90
AND
PROUD
OF IT

summersdale

90 AND PROUD OF IT

Summersdale Publishers Ltd
46 West Street
Chichester
West Sussex
PO19 1RP
UK

www.summersdale.com

Printed and bound in the Czech Republic

ISBN: 978-1-84953-694-3

Substantial discounts on bulk quantities of Summersdale books are available to corporations, professional associations and other organisations. For details contact Nicky Douglas by telephone: +44 (0) 1243 756902, fax: +44 (0) 1243 786300 or email: nicky@summersdale.com.

TO......................................

FROM......................................

CONTENTS

ANOTHER YEAR OLDER

YOU ARE NEVER TOO OLD TO SET ANOTHER GOAL OR TO DREAM A NEW DREAM.

C. S. Lewis

I WANT TO LIVE TO BE 120. THAT'S WHEN I WILL START WORRYING ABOUT MY AGE.

Helena Christensen

IF THINGS GET BETTER
WITH AGE THEN YOU
ARE APPROACHING
MAGNIFICENT.

Anonymous

I INTEND TO
LIVE FOREVER,
OR DIE TRYING.

Groucho Marx

LIVE YOUR LIFE AND FORGET YOUR AGE.

Norman Vincent Peale

A BIRTHDAY IS JUST THE
FIRST DAY OF ANOTHER
365-DAY JOURNEY
AROUND THE SUN.
ENJOY THE TRIP.

Anonymous

NO ONE IS SO OLD AS TO
THINK THAT HE CANNOT
LIVE ONE MORE YEAR.

Cicero

THE OLDER THE FIDDLE, THE SWEETER THE TUNE.

English proverb

YOU CAN'T TURN BACK
THE CLOCK, BUT YOU CAN
WIND IT UP AGAIN.

Bonnie Prudden

AGE IS SOMETHING THAT DOESN'T MATTER, UNLESS YOU ARE A CHEESE.

Luis Buñuel

YOU CAN LIVE TO
BE 100 IF YOU GIVE UP
ALL THE THINGS THAT
MAKE YOU WANT TO
LIVE TO BE 100.

Woody Allen

A TRUE FRIEND REMEMBERS YOUR BIRTHDAY BUT NOT YOUR AGE.

Anonymous

BIRTHDAYS ARE GOOD
FOR YOU. STATISTICS
SHOW THAT THE PEOPLE
WHO HAVE THE MOST
LIVE THE LONGEST.

Larry Lorenzoni

FOR ALL THE ADVANCES
IN MEDICINE, THERE IS
STILL NO CURE FOR THE
COMMON BIRTHDAY.

John Glenn

PLEAS'D TO LOOK
FORWARD, PLEAS'D TO
LOOK BEHIND, AND COUNT
EACH BIRTHDAY WITH A
GRATEFUL MIND.

Alexander Pope

STOP WORRYING ABOUT
THE POTHOLES IN THE
ROAD AND CELEBRATE
THE JOURNEY!

Anonymous

AS THIS AUSPICIOUS DAY
BEGAN THE RACE
OF EV'RY VIRTUE JOIN'D
WITH EV'RY GRACE;
MAY YOU, WHO OWN THEM,
WELCOME ITS RETURN,
TILL EXCELLENCE, LIKE
YOURS, AGAIN IS BORN.

Francis Jeffrey

I DIDN'T GET OLD
ON PURPOSE, IT JUST
HAPPENED. IF YOU'RE
LUCKY, IT COULD
HAPPEN TO YOU.

Andy Rooney

AGE IS JUST A
NUMBER. IT'S TOTALLY
IRRELEVANT UNLESS, OF
COURSE, YOU HAPPEN TO
BE A BOTTLE OF WINE.

Joan Collins

THE FIRST 100 YEARS ARE THE HARDEST.

Wilson Mizner

AN OLD-TIMER IS ONE
WHO REMEMBERS
WHEN WE COUNTED OUR
BLESSINGS INSTEAD OF
OUR CALORIES.

Anonymous

THE GREAT THING ABOUT GETTING OLDER IS THAT YOU DON'T LOSE ALL THE OTHER AGES YOU'VE BEEN.

Madeleine L'Engle

JUST
WHAT
I ALWAYS
WANTED

YOU KNOW YOU'RE
GETTING OLD WHEN THE
CANDLES COST MORE
THAN THE CAKE.

Bob Hope

YESTERDAY IS HISTORY,
TOMORROW IS A MYSTERY,
BUT TODAY IS A GIFT.
THAT IS WHY IT IS
CALLED THE PRESENT.

Eleanor Roosevelt

IF INSTEAD OF A GEM,
OR EVEN A FLOWER,
WE SHOULD CAST THE
GIFT OF A LOVING
THOUGHT INTO THE
HEART OF A FRIEND,
THAT WOULD BE GIVING
AS THE ANGELS GIVE.

George MacDonald

THERE ARE 364 DAYS
WHEN YOU MIGHT
GET UN-BIRTHDAY
PRESENTS... AND ONLY
ONE FOR BIRTHDAY
PRESENTS, YOU KNOW.

Lewis Carroll

A GIFT WITH A KIND COUNTENANCE IS A DOUBLE PRESENT.

Proverb

NOBODY CAN BE UNCHEERED WITH A BALLOON.

A. A. Milne

SURPRISE IS THE
GREATEST GIFT WHICH
LIFE CAN GRANT US.

Boris Pasternak

THE MORE CANDLES
YOU HAVE ON A CAKE,
THE BIGGER THE WISH
YOU MAKE.

Anonymous

EACH DAY COMES BEARING ITS OWN GIFTS. UNTIE THE RIBBONS.

Ruth Ann Schabacker

WHY IS A BIRTHDAY CAKE THE ONLY FOOD YOU CAN BLOW ON AND SPIT ON AND EVERYBODY RUSHES TO GET A PIECE?

Bobby Kelton

A HUG IS THE PERFECT
GIFT — ONE SIZE FITS
ALL AND NOBODY MINDS
IF YOU EXCHANGE IT.

Irvin Ball

EVERY BIRTHDAY, EVERY
CELEBRATION ENDS WITH
SOMETHING SWEET,
A CAKE, AND PEOPLE
REMEMBER. IT'S ALL
ABOUT THE MEMORIES.

Buddy Valastro

GRIN
AND
BEAR
IT

AGEING SEEMS TO BE
THE ONLY AVAILABLE WAY
TO LIVE A LONG LIFE.

Kitty O'Neill Collins

WHEN IT COMES TO AGE
WE'RE ALL IN THE SAME
BOAT, ONLY SOME OF US
HAVE BEEN ABOARD A
LITTLE LONGER.

Leo Probst

OLD MEN ARE FOND OF
GIVING GOOD ADVICE, TO
CONSOLE THEMSELVES
FOR BEING NO LONGER
IN A POSITION TO GIVE
BAD EXAMPLES.

François de La Rochefoucauld

EVEN IF THERE'S
SNOW ON THE ROOF,
IT DOESN'T MEAN THE
FIRE HAS GONE OUT IN
THE FURNACE.

Anonymous

DO NOT WORRY ABOUT
AVOIDING TEMPTATION.
AS YOU GROW OLDER IT
WILL AVOID YOU.

Joey Adams

OLD AGE IS NO PLACE
FOR SISSIES.

Bette Davis

I'M LIKE A
GOOD CHEESE.
I'M JUST
GETTING MOULDY
ENOUGH TO BE
INTERESTING.

Paul Newman

I ADVISE YOU TO GO
ON LIVING SOLELY TO
ENRAGE THOSE WHO
ARE PAYING YOUR
ANNUITIES. IT IS THE
ONLY PLEASURE I
HAVE LEFT.

Oscar Wilde

YOUTH IS A WONDERFUL
THING. WHAT A CRIME TO
WASTE IT ON CHILDREN.

George Bernard Shaw

I WAS ALWAYS TAUGHT TO
RESPECT MY ELDERS AND
I'VE NOW REACHED THE
AGE WHEN I DON'T HAVE
ANYBODY TO RESPECT.

George Burns

GETTING OLD IS A BIT
LIKE GETTING DRUNK;
EVERYONE ELSE LOOKS
BRILLIANT.

Billy Connolly

I STILL HAVE A FULL
DECK; I JUST SHUFFLE
SLOWER NOW.

Anonymous

AGE IS AN ISSUE OF
MIND OVER MATTER.
IF YOU DON'T MIND, IT
DOESN'T MATTER.

Mark Twain

NO WISE MAN EVER WISHED TO BE YOUNGER.

Jonathan Swift

THE GOOD THING ABOUT BEING OLD IS NOT BEING YOUNG.

Stephen Richards

OLD AGE IS THE MOST
UNEXPECTED OF ALL
THE THINGS THAT CAN
HAPPEN TO A MAN.

Leon Trotsky

OLD AGE IS AN
EXCELLENT TIME FOR
OUTRAGE. MY GOAL IS
TO SAY OR DO AT LEAST
ONE OUTRAGEOUS THING
EVERY WEEK.

Maggie Kuhn

WHEN I WAS A BOY THE DEAD SEA WAS ONLY SICK.

George Burns

DO A
LITTLE
DANCE,
MAKE A
LITTLE
LOVE

I CELEBRATE MYSELF, AND SING MYSELF.

Walt Whitman

YOU ONLY LIVE ONCE, BUT IF YOU DO IT RIGHT, ONCE IS ENOUGH.

Mae West

CHERISH ALL YOUR
HAPPY MOMENTS: THEY
MAKE A FINE CUSHION
FOR OLD AGE.

Christopher Morley

ONE OF THE BEST PARTS
OF GROWING OLDER?
YOU CAN FLIRT ALL
YOU LIKE SINCE YOU'VE
BECOME HARMLESS.

Liz Smith

LET US CELEBRATE THE
OCCASION WITH WINE
AND SWEET WORDS.

Plautus

THE OTHER DAY A
MAN ASKED ME WHAT I
THOUGHT WAS THE BEST
TIME OF LIFE. 'WHY,' I
ANSWERED WITHOUT A
THOUGHT, 'NOW.'

David Grayson

LIFE IS JUST ONE GRAND, SWEET SONG, SO START THE MUSIC.

Ronald Reagan

I ALWAYS MAKE A
POINT OF STARTING
THE DAY... WITH
CHAMPAGNE. IT GOES
STRAIGHT TO THE HEART
AND CHEERS ONE UP.

John Mortimer

WITH MIRTH AND
LAUGHTER LET OLD
WRINKLES COME.

William Shakespeare

OLD AGE AND
TREACHERY WILL
ALWAYS BEAT YOUTH
AND EXUBERANCE.

David Mamet

THE OLDER ONE GROWS, THE MORE ONE LIKES INDECENCY.

Virginia Woolf

GROWING OLD IS
COMPULSORY —
GROWING UP IS
OPTIONAL.

Bob Monkhouse

NOBODY LOVES LIFE
LIKE HIM THAT'S
GROWING OLD.

Sophocles

THE LONGER I LIVE
THE MORE BEAUTIFUL
LIFE BECOMES.

Frank Lloyd Wright

IT'S IMPORTANT TO HAVE A TWINKLE IN YOUR WRINKLE.

Anonymous

YOUNG

AT

HEART

THE GREAT SECRET
THAT ALL OLD PEOPLE
SHARE IS THAT YOU
REALLY HAVEN'T
CHANGED... YOUR BODY
CHANGES, BUT YOU
DON'T CHANGE AT ALL.

Doris Lessing

TO KEEP THE HEART
UNWRINKLED, TO BE
HOPEFUL, KINDLY,
CHEERFUL, REVERENT
— THAT IS TO TRIUMPH
OVER OLD AGE.

Thomas B. Aldrich

OLD AGE IS NOT JUST FOR GROWN-UPS.

Benny Bellamacina

WHITE HAIR OFTEN
COVERS THE HEAD, BUT
THE HEART THAT HOLDS
IT IS EVER YOUNG.

Honoré de Balzac

YOUTH WOULD BE AN
IDEAL STATE IF IT CAME
A LITTLE LATER IN LIFE.

H. H. Asquith

THE IMPORTANT
THING... IS NOT HOW
MANY YEARS IN YOUR
LIFE, BUT HOW MUCH
LIFE IN YOUR YEARS!

Edward Stieglitz

TO WIN BACK MY YOUTH...
THERE IS NOTHING I
WOULDN'T DO — EXCEPT
TAKE EXERCISE, GET UP
EARLY, OR BE A USEFUL
MEMBER OF THE
COMMUNITY.

Oscar Wilde

AGE DOES NOT
DIMINISH THE EXTREME
DISAPPOINTMENT OF
HAVING A SCOOP OF ICE
CREAM FALL FROM
THE CONE.

Jim Fiebig

INSIDE EVERY
OLDER PERSON IS A
YOUNGER PERSON
— WONDERING
WHAT THE HELL
HAPPENED.

Cora Harvey Armstrong

YOU'RE ONLY AS YOUNG
AS THE LAST TIME YOU
CHANGED YOUR MIND.

Timothy Leary

OLD AGE IS LIKE
EVERYTHING ELSE.
TO MAKE A SUCCESS OF
IT, YOU'VE GOT TO
START YOUNG.

Theodore Roosevelt

THE SECRET TO
STAYING YOUNG IS TO
LIVE HONESTLY, EAT
SLOWLY, AND LIE
ABOUT YOUR AGE.

Lucille Ball

EVERYONE IS THE AGE OF THEIR HEART.

Guatemalan proverb

IT TAKES A LONG TIME
TO BECOME YOUNG.

Pablo Picasso

OLDER
AND
WISER?

WHEN YOU GET RID
OF ALL THE OLDER
PEOPLE, YOU GET RID
OF ALL THE WISDOM.

Terraine Francois

KEEP THE ENTHUSIASM
OF YOUR YOUTH AND
TREASURE THE WISDOM
OF OLD AGE.

Lailah Gifty Akita

NOW THAT I'M 91, AS OPPOSED TO BEING 90, I'M MUCH WISER.

Betty White

WISDOM DOESN'T
NECESSARILY COME
WITH AGE. SOMETIMES
AGE JUST SHOWS UP
ALL BY ITSELF.

Tom Wilson

THE YOUNG SOW WILD OATS. THE OLD GROW SAGE.

Winston Churchill

I'M NOT YOUNG
ENOUGH TO KNOW
EVERYTHING.

J. M. Barrie

THE MORE SAND
HAS ESCAPED FROM
THE HOURGLASS OF OUR
LIFE, THE CLEARER
WE SHOULD SEE
THROUGH IT.

Jean Paul

IF I HAD MY LIFE TO
LIVE OVER AGAIN,
I'D MAKE THE SAME
MISTAKES, ONLY SOONER.

Tallulah Bankhead

AS YOU GROW OLDER,
YOU LEARN TO
UNDERSTAND LIFE
A LITTLE BETTER.

Solomon Burke

ALL LIFE IS AN
EXPERIMENT. THE
MORE EXPERIMENTS YOU
MAKE THE BETTER.

Ralph Waldo Emerson

IF YOU CAN SPEND A
PERFECTLY USELESS
AFTERNOON IN A
PERFECTLY USELESS
MANNER, YOU HAVE
LEARNED HOW TO LIVE.

Lin Yutang

TO KNOW HOW TO GROW
OLD IS THE MASTERWORK
OF WISDOM, AND ONE OF
THE MOST DIFFICULT
CHAPTERS IN THE GREAT
ART OF LIVING.

Henri-Frédéric Amiel

THEY TOLD ME IF
I GOT OLDER I'D GET
WISER. IN THAT CASE
I MUST BE A GENIUS.

George Burns

IT'S WHAT YOU LEARN AFTER YOU KNOW IT ALL THAT COUNTS.

John Wooden

NO MAN IS EVER OLD ENOUGH TO KNOW BETTER.

Holbrook Jackson

AS ONE GROWS OLDER,
ONE BECOMES WISER AND
MORE FOOLISH.

François de La Rochefoucauld

LIVE, LOVE AND LAST

IF I'D KNOWN I
WAS GOING TO LIVE
THIS LONG, I'D HAVE
TAKEN BETTER CARE
OF MYSELF.

Eubie Blake

YOUTH DISSERVES;
MIDDLE AGE CONSERVES;
OLD AGE PRESERVES.

Martin H. Fischer

YOU CAN'T HELP
GETTING OLDER,
BUT YOU DON'T HAVE
TO GET OLD.

George Burns

THERE IS NO OLD AGE.
THERE IS, AS THERE
ALWAYS WAS, JUST YOU.

Carol Matthau

THE GOOD OLD DAYS ARE NOW.

Tom Clancy

OLD PEOPLE AREN'T
EXEMPT FROM HAVING
FUN AND DANCING.

Liz Smith

THE ABILITY TO
LAUGH, ESPECIALLY AT
OURSELVES, KEEPS THE
HEART LIGHT AND THE
MIND YOUNG.

Anonymous

A COMFORTABLE
OLD AGE IS THE
REWARD OF A
WELL-SPENT
YOUTH.

Maurice Chevalier

AGE, LIKE DISTANCE, LENDS A DOUBLE CHARM.

Oliver Wendell Holmes Jr

FEW THINGS ARE
MORE DELIGHTFUL
THAN GRANDCHILDREN
FIGHTING OVER
YOUR LAP.

Doug Larson

I LOVE EVERYTHING
THAT'S OLD: OLD
FRIENDS, OLD TIMES,
OLD MANNERS, OLD
BOOKS, OLD WINE.

Oliver Goldsmith

HE WHO LAUGHS, LASTS!

Mary Pettibone Poole

MY ADVICE FOR LIFE:
DANCE AND SING YOUR
SONG WHILE THE PARTY
IS STILL ON.

Rasheed Ogunlaru

HE DRANK TO LIFE, TO
ALL IT HAD BEEN, TO
WHAT IT WAS, TO WHAT
IT WOULD BE.

Sean O'Casey

ILLS,
PILLS
AND
TWINGES

AS YOU GET OLDER
THREE THINGS HAPPEN.
THE FIRST IS YOUR
MEMORY GOES, AND I
CAN'T REMEMBER THE
OTHER TWO...

Norman Wisdom

IF WRINKLES MUST
BE WRITTEN UPON
OUR BROWS, LET THEM
NOT BE WRITTEN UPON
THE HEART. THE SPIRIT
SHOULD NEVER
GROW OLD.

James A. Garfield

I DON'T FEEL OLD.
I DON'T FEEL
ANYTHING TILL
NOON. THAT'S
WHEN IT'S TIME
FOR MY NAP.

Bob Hope

OLDER PEOPLE
SHOULDN'T EAT HEALTH
FOOD, THEY NEED ALL
THE PRESERVATIVES
THEY CAN GET.

Robert Orben

WRINKLES SHOULD
MERELY INDICATE
WHERE THE SMILES
HAVE BEEN.

Mark Twain

I DON'T NEED YOU TO
REMIND ME OF MY AGE.
I HAVE A BLADDER TO DO
THAT FOR ME.

Stephen Fry

I'LL KEEP SWIVELLING
MY HIPS UNTIL THEY
NEED REPLACING.

Tom Jones

THE EASIEST WAY
TO DIMINISH THE
APPEARANCE OF
WRINKLES IS TO KEEP
YOUR GLASSES OFF
WHEN YOU LOOK IN
THE MIRROR.

Joan Rivers

DON'T LET AGEING GET
YOU DOWN. IT'S TOO
HARD TO GET BACK UP.

John Wagner

AGE SELDOM ARRIVES SMOOTHLY OR QUICKLY. IT'S MORE OFTEN A SUCCESSION OF JERKS.

Jean Rhys

YEARS MAY WRINKLE
THE SKIN, BUT TO
GIVE UP ENTHUSIASM
WRINKLES THE SOUL.

Samuel Ullman

LAUGHTER DOESN'T REQUIRE TEETH.

Bill Newton

DON'T RETOUCH
MY WRINKLES...
I WOULD NOT WANT IT
TO BE THOUGHT THAT
I HAD LIVED FOR ALL
THESE YEARS WITHOUT
SOMETHING TO SHOW
FOR IT.

Queen Elizabeth, The Queen Mother

CHIN UP, CHEST OUT

I'M NOT SURE THAT OLD AGE ISN'T THE BEST PART OF LIFE.

C. S. Lewis

WHEN GRACE IS JOINED
WITH WRINKLES, IT IS
ADORABLE. THERE IS AN
UNSPEAKABLE DAWN IN
HAPPY OLD AGE.

Victor Hugo

YOUTH IS THE GIFT OF NATURE, BUT AGE IS A WORK OF ART.

Garson Kanin

I'M LIKE OLD WINE. THEY
DON'T BRING ME OUT
VERY OFTEN, BUT I'M
WELL PRESERVED.

Rose Kennedy

TIME IS A DRESSMAKER
SPECIALISING IN
ALTERATIONS.

Faith Baldwin

WE TURN NOT OLDER WITH YEARS, BUT NEWER EVERY DAY.

Emily Dickinson

OLD AGE:
THE CROWN OF LIFE.

Cicero

MY IDEA OF HELL IS TO BE YOUNG AGAIN.

Marge Piercy

BECAUSE OF YOUR SMILE, YOU MAKE LIFE MORE BEAUTIFUL.

Thích Nhât Hạnh

IT'S NOT HOW OLD
YOU ARE, BUT HOW
YOU ARE OLD.

Marie Dressler

OUR WRINKLES ARE
OUR MEDALS OF THE
PASSAGE OF LIFE.

Lauren Hutton

PERHAPS ONE
HAS TO BE VERY OLD
BEFORE ONE LEARNS
HOW TO BE AMUSED
RATHER THAN SHOCKED.

Pearl S. Buck

IF YOU SURVIVE LONG
ENOUGH, YOU'RE
REVERED — RATHER
LIKE AN OLD BUILDING.

Katharine Hepburn

THE MORE YOU
PRAISE AND CELEBRATE
YOUR LIFE, THE MORE
THERE IS IN LIFE TO
CELEBRATE.

Oprah Winfrey

IN OUR DREAMS WE
ARE ALWAYS YOUNG.

Sarah Louise Delany

WE ARE NOT LIMITED BY OUR OLD AGE; WE ARE LIBERATED BY IT.

Stu Mittleman

MAY YOU LIVE ALL THE DAYS OF YOUR LIFE.

Jonathan Swift

THE ELDERLY DON'T
DRIVE THAT BADLY;
THEY'RE JUST THE ONLY
ONES WITH TIME TO DO
THE SPEED LIMIT.

Jason Love

IT IS TRUE YOU ARE
GENTLY SHOULDERED
OFF THE STAGE, BUT
THEN YOU ARE GIVEN
SUCH A COMFORTABLE
FRONT STALL AS
SPECTATOR.

Jane Harrison on old age

OLD AGE HAS ITS
PLEASURES WHICH,
THOUGH DIFFERENT,
ARE NOT LESS THAN THE
PLEASURES OF YOUTH.

W. Somerset Maugham

YOU DON'T GET OLDER, YOU GET BETTER.

Shirley Bassey

Meet Esme!

Our feathered friend Esme loves finding perfect
quotes for the perfect occasion, and is almost as
good at collecting them as she is at collecting twigs
for her nest. She's always full of joy and happiness,
singing her messages of goodwill in this series
of uplifting, heart-warming books.

Follow Esme on Twitter at **@EsmeTheBird**.

For more information about our books,
find us on Facebook at **Summersdale Publishers**
and follow us on Twitter at **@Summersdale**.

www.summersdale.com